THE Great Rubbish Mountain

Colin Walker

CollinsEducational
An imprint of HarperCollins*Publishers*

Contents

Introduction

This year each person in your household will use about 160 cans and 160 bottles, 45 kilograms of plastics, and all the wood fibre, paper and cardboard produced from two large trees. Fabric will be used to make clothes; leather and rubber will be used to produce shoes and belts. Some of us will use petrol, oil, metals and paint.

Chemicals may be used, in things such as household cleaners or sprays on the food we eat, or in factories that make various goods.

We are all *consumers* of a great range of things that have been grown, made or bought. We are also the people that build mountains of rubbish. The more things we use, the more rubbish we create.

Britain produces a rather large rubbish mountain — about twenty-eight million tonnes every year!

All this rubbish has to be taken away from our homes, schools, offices and factories and dumped somewhere. Many towns and cities are running out of room to dump things. In some places, rubbish has to be carried long distances, and this is expensive.

Litter, the rubbish that people have discarded improperly, can be seen everywhere: plastic bags, foam plastic, plastic containers and lids; glass bottles and broken glass; cigarette butts, paper and wrappers; metal cans; and food. If you walk along a lake front or the seashore or your street, you will see many kinds of litter polluting your environment. All this has to be cleaned up and removed, too.

Many types of rubbish will *decompose* or rot away naturally, but this takes time.

Most things can break down naturally — but some materials need a very long time!

Fruit peel	2–5 weeks
Cigarette butts	1–5 years
Woollen socks	1–5 years
Plastic-coated paper	5 years
Plastic bags	10–20 years
Plastic film containers	20–30 years
Nylon fabric	30–40 years
Rubber boot soles	50–80 years
Aluminium cans	80–100 years

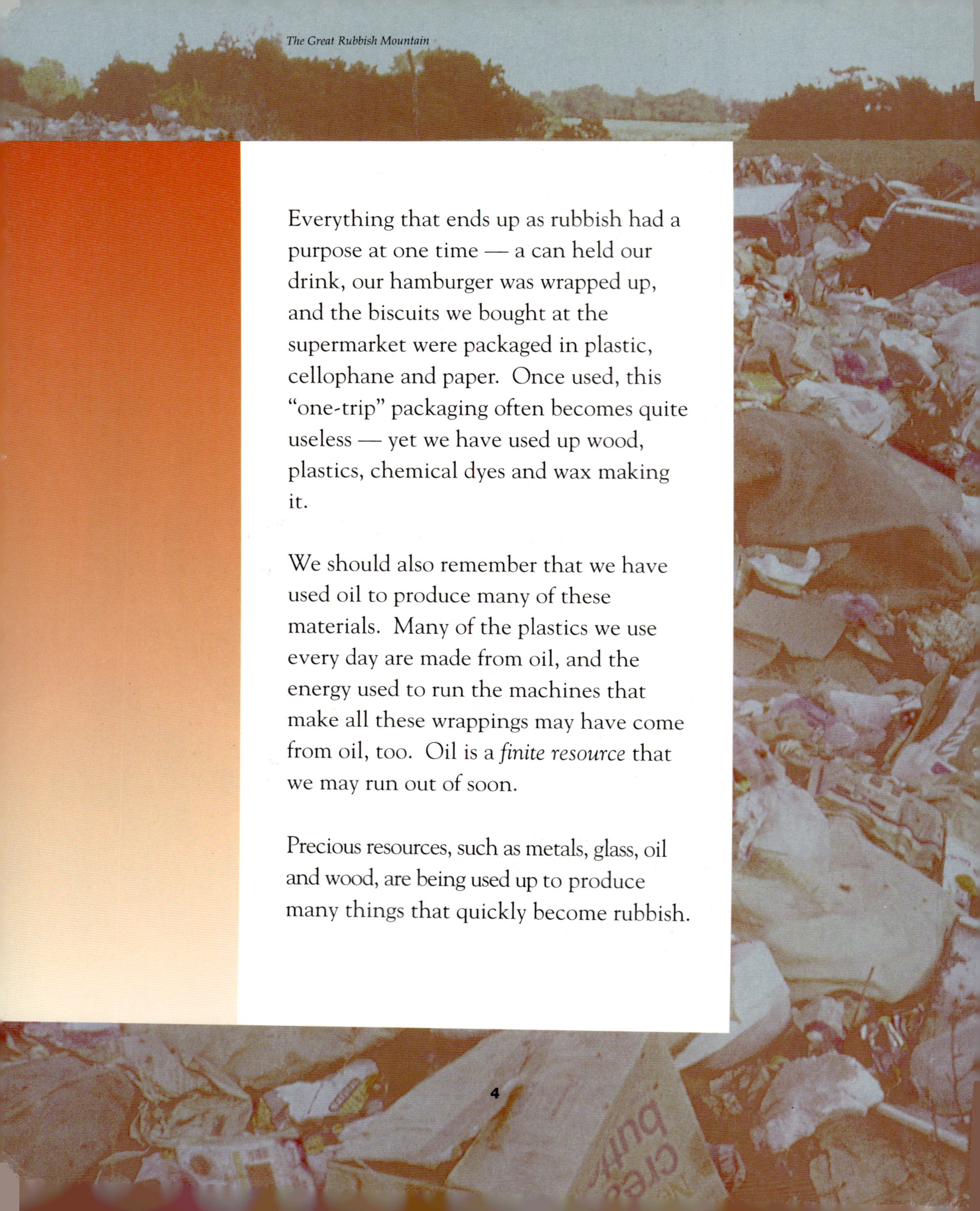

Everything that ends up as rubbish had a purpose at one time — a can held our drink, our hamburger was wrapped up, and the biscuits we bought at the supermarket were packaged in plastic, cellophane and paper. Once used, this "one-trip" packaging often becomes quite useless — yet we have used up wood, plastics, chemical dyes and wax making it.

We should also remember that we have used oil to produce many of these materials. Many of the plastics we use every day are made from oil, and the energy used to run the machines that make all these wrappings may have come from oil, too. Oil is a *finite resource* that we may run out of soon.

Precious resources, such as metals, glass, oil and wood, are being used up to produce many things that quickly become rubbish.

We all use paper — but did you know that this year you will use about 140 kilograms of it? It makes up one-fifth of all the rubbish that is thrown out of your household every week.

Think about the answers to these questions:

How often do you use both sides of a page?
Do you have a place where you can keep half-used paper for further use later on?
Do you use paper tissues or cloth handkerchiefs?
When you go shopping, do you buy items with simple or no packaging?
Do you buy your milk or fruit juice in cartons or bottles?

It costs 50–80% less to build a factory to process old paper into new than it does to build a mill that makes new paper from wood.

Recycling factories also produce only half as much air and water pollution as mills making new paper from wood.

In the Netherlands and Japan, over half of the paper mountain is recycled. Other countries are starting to recycle, but most of it is still being dumped.

After being used, many paper products can be easily *recycled,* yet so many of them are dumped. Paper products, including newspapers, magazines and cardboard, can be collected, sorted and sometimes even sold for income.

Saving paper saves 20 percent of the space needed in rubbish tips. It means fewer trees need to be cut down, and this can sometimes mean that less land *erosion* occurs.

Compost

Almost half of the bulk of each week's domestic rubbish is made up of *biodegradable* vegetable and fruit leftovers. These leftovers can be broken down by bacteria into plant *nutrients* if they are composted.

When spread over the garden, this compost recycles nutrients to plants, trees and shrubs. It can prevent weeds from growing and can also conserve water in the ground.

- *In Japan, vegetable and fruit leftovers are processed into commercial* fertilisers.
- *In India, over a million* biogas *plants turn vegetable and fruit waste into valuable gas that can be used for cooking and heating.*
- *Biogas plants also produce ash that is used as a fertiliser, save many thousands of trees from ending up as firewood, and keep villages hygienic, as rubbish is put to a good use.*

Cans

Most of the cans we use are made from aluminium, which is created from the mineral called bauxite, mined mainly in Australia and Jamaica. Aluminium is a wonderfully adaptable metal. It is hard, long-lasting, rust-proof and easily shaped — which means it is used for many things ranging from buildings, machinery and electrical goods to cans and containers.

- *Every one of the millions and millions of aluminium cans we use each year can be recycled.*
- *By encouraging recycling, we can reduce mining and the spoiling of the landscape.*
- *We can also cut down on the huge amounts of electricity needed to produce aluminium from bauxite.*

Collection centres for these cans are becoming more common — you may have one at home and near your school.

"Tin" cans are actually made from steel, lined with tin. They often have an aluminium top or base. To recycle a container made of three metals, each metal must be separated. As each metal has different properties, such as melting points, this can be difficult. Separation often involves the use of caustic soda, which is a dangerous toxic substance.

Perhaps it is time to think about whether these types of cans are still needed. There may be alternatives that are cheaper to make and easier to recycle. After all, the world's supply of tin could run out in five years!

South Australia recycles 90% of its cans, Japan recycles 50% of its cans, and New Zealand recycles 20% of its cans.

Plastics

The first plastics were invented last century using the casein in cows' milk, and the first artificial plastic was called Bakelite. Since then, plastic rubbish, which makes up nearly two-thirds of beach litter and 10 percent of domestic rubbish, has been increasing in volume.

Plastics have many desirable properties.

- *They do not rust.*
- *They are easily formed into different shapes.*
- *They are extremely long-lasting.*
- *They can be made rigid or flexible.*
- *They can be porous or non-porous.*
- *They can be coloured, opaque, translucent or clear.*
- *They are ideal for many uses, ranging from drainpipes, sink tops, furniture, and car parts to the many packing and wrapping materials we see when we go shopping.*

Each day, the world's ships dump 640,000 plastic items into the sea.

In 1975, about 135,000 tonnes of plastic fishing gear was lost or dumped at sea.

There are over thirty different kinds of plastic in use today.

The desirable features of plastics can also make disposing of them more difficult.

Most plastics are not biodegradable, but some plastics are being invented that will break down through the action of sunlight. These plastics are *photo-degradable*. Photo-degradable plastics will prevent the deaths of many sea animals. At present, plastics such as nylon nets, wrapping string, plastic bags, and the rings that hold six-packs of drinks together often strangle or choke the creatures of the sea — whales, dolphins, turtles, seals and fish are all in danger.

Scientists are trying to find new plastics that will break down completely and not even leave particles behind to cause pollution. In future, plastics might be produced from natural materials, such as wheat or rice stalks, which would not cause pollution problems.

Polystyrene plastics are light, shock resistant, and cheap to produce, but they are also difficult to dispose of. Making polystyrene can also release dangerous chemicals into the environment, and its bulk takes up precious space in rubbish dumps.

Many fast-food restaurants are replacing polystyrene in their burger containers and are looking for other things to use in their disposable plates and coffee cups. Customers can also play their part by helping in schemes to keep the waste plastic, paper, and waxed containers separate for recycling.

Soft drinks and fruit juices are available in a variety of soft drink containers. Glass bottles are both reusable and recyclable. Juice boxes are not reusable; and because they combine cardboard, aluminium and plastic, they are only partially biodegradable, and difficult to recycle. Plastic bottles made of PET (polyethylene terephthalate) cannot be reused and are not biodegradable, but they can be recycled.

Recycled plastics can be made into products such as filling for sleeping bags and pillows, building materials, crash barriers on roads and water pipes. In Japan, a synthetic "timber" is made from recycled plastic. Walls, paving blocks, street signs and plant containers are just some of the other uses recycled plastic can be put to. Over 80 percent of plastic can be recycled!

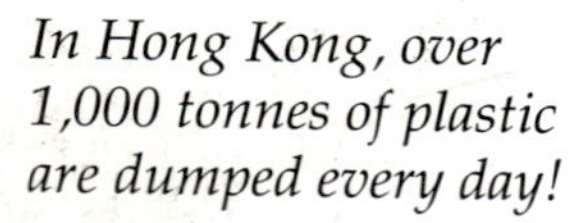

In Hong Kong, over 1,000 tonnes of plastic are dumped every day!

Glass

Glass is much simpler to recycle than plastics, and glass bottles can be used up to sixty times. After the last "trip", the glass can still be recycled and used. Many glass manufacturers mix up to a quarter of old glass with the silica sand, soda or limestone used to make new glass. Other glass factories can process old glass into completely new glass and save energy costs by making it this way. This process also produces less air pollution than the traditional way of making glass.

For some bottled goods, there is a deposit on the bottle, which is refundable when swapped for another. The higher the deposit, the more bottles are returned for refilling. This means cheaper costs — which means *you* pay less.

Many of the things we buy are in non-returnable bottles. This only means it is not economical to return them to their original factory. The bottles can still be recycled.

Industrial Waste

If dumped together, some industrial wastes, such as hydrochloric acid, can become gases that are able to kill us and other living things. Chemical reactions in mixed dumps can sometimes cause fires, which release even more toxic fumes into the atmosphere. Oils, timber preservatives, and many other chemicals can *leach* into the ground, killing the animals and plants that live in rivers, streams and lakes and polluting our water supplies.

Dumps for these kinds of wastes can be made safe if they are put in the right place. Layers of clay and other materials can keep wastes from seeping through the ground. Some dangerous materials can be burned safely, using special chimney filters that prevent poisonous gases from entering the air. Energy is also produced and can be used — in one town in Denmark, a waste incinerator provides 35 percent of the town's heating needs.

Other industrial wastes can be reused. Oil can be re-refined and used again. Metals, like the lead in batteries, can be reused, and chemicals can also be cleaned and reused. The cost of doing these things can be high to start with, but once the systems have been set up, it becomes cheaper and cheaper over time.

Short-term ways of disposing of waste generally mean long-term problems for someone else, somewhere else.

In 1987, the sea freighter Pelicano *was loaded with 14,000 tonnes of toxic ash to unload at another port. For two years, it roamed the oceans without finding anywhere that would allow it to unload its poisonous cargo. Finally, it dumped part of its load off the Haitian coast and the rest at an unknown port.*

The dumpship Nerva *discharges 500 tonnes of dangerous waste off the Spanish coast every day, while the burn-ship* Volcanus *incinerates waste at sea.*

Getting rid of waste in these ways only moves the pollution from one place to another, or changes the form of the pollution.

We Need Action

We are living on a planet that is becoming more and more polluted with waste and trash. Disposing of the great rubbish mountain is a problem. Most of the rubbish once had a good use, so we cannot simply stop making these things. However, the same technology that helped to create these things for people to use can teach us how to recycle them or convert them into goods for other uses.

Everyone needs to be aware of the problems and help find answers. When we are buying goods, we can look carefully at the packaging as well as the product. We can think about whether the packaging is necessary or can be easily recycled. We can encourage factories and shops to package their goods in a better way by buying products that are packaged well.

Everyone can become involved in recycling — by separating different types of waste, by using local recycling bins, and by composting household wastes.

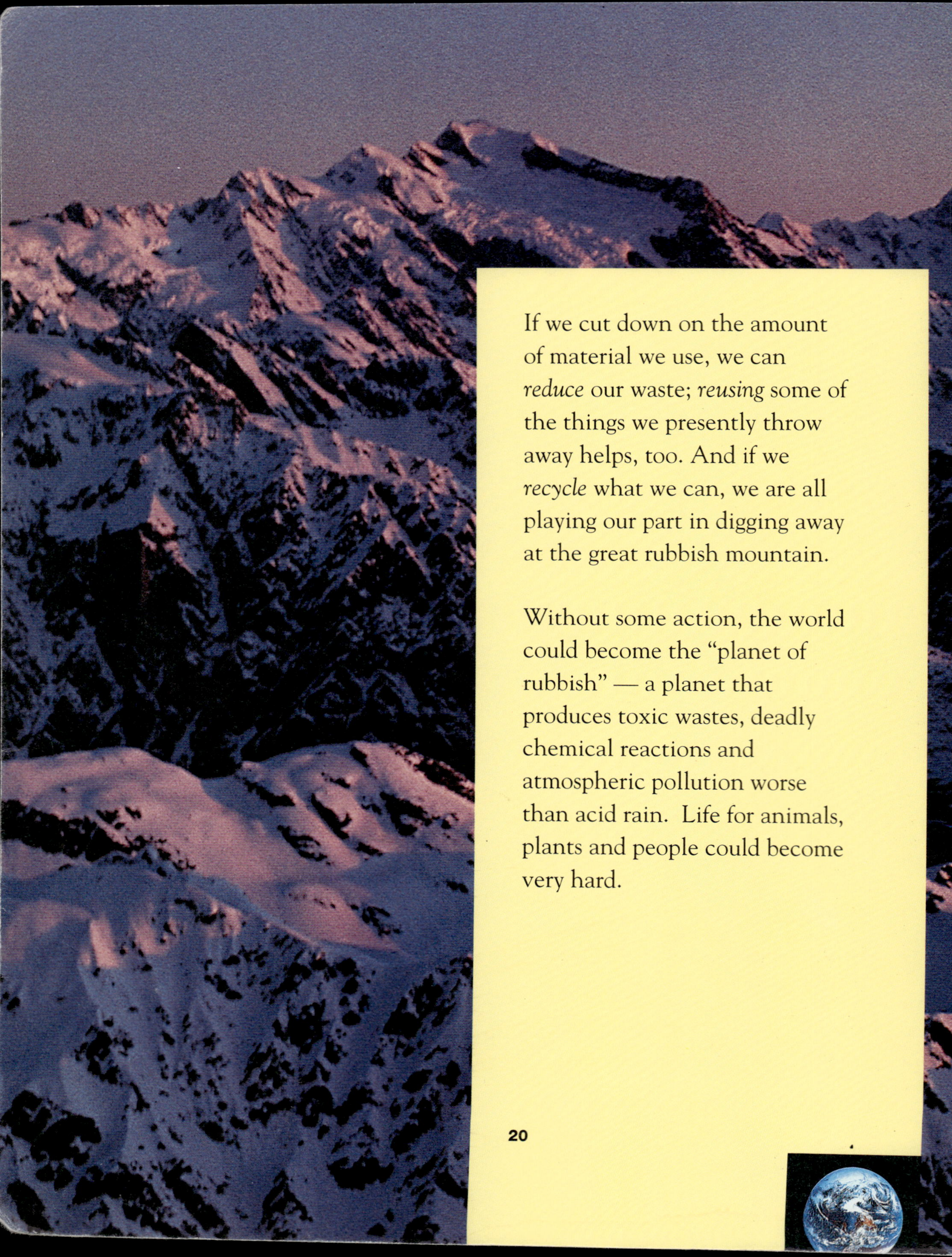

If we cut down on the amount of material we use, we can *reduce* our waste; *reusing* some of the things we presently throw away helps, too. And if we *recycle* what we can, we are all playing our part in digging away at the great rubbish mountain.

Without some action, the world could become the "planet of rubbish" — a planet that produces toxic wastes, deadly chemical reactions and atmospheric pollution worse than acid rain. Life for animals, plants and people could become very hard.

Glossary

biodegradable — able to be broken down by bacteria.

biogas — a gas produced from vegetable waste and used as a fuel.

casein — a protein found in milk, used in the production of cheese, and originally in the production of plastic.

consumer — anyone who uses up a resource.

erosion — the wearing away and movement of soil or rocks by wind and water.

fertiliser — natural or artificial chemicals that plants need to grow strong.

finite resource — a resource is something that is available to be used for a particular purpose; a finite resource is one that we only have limited supplies of.

leach — to soak or seep through a porous substance.

nutrients — the chemicals and minerals that are used by plants to grow.

opaque — not letting light through, or not able to be seen through.

photo-degradable — able to be broken down into simpler parts by sunlight.

porous — filled with tiny holes that fluids can seep through.

recycle — to use a product again after it has been used for its main or first purpose.

synthetic — artificial, not natural.

toxic — poisonous.

translucent — letting light through.

Index